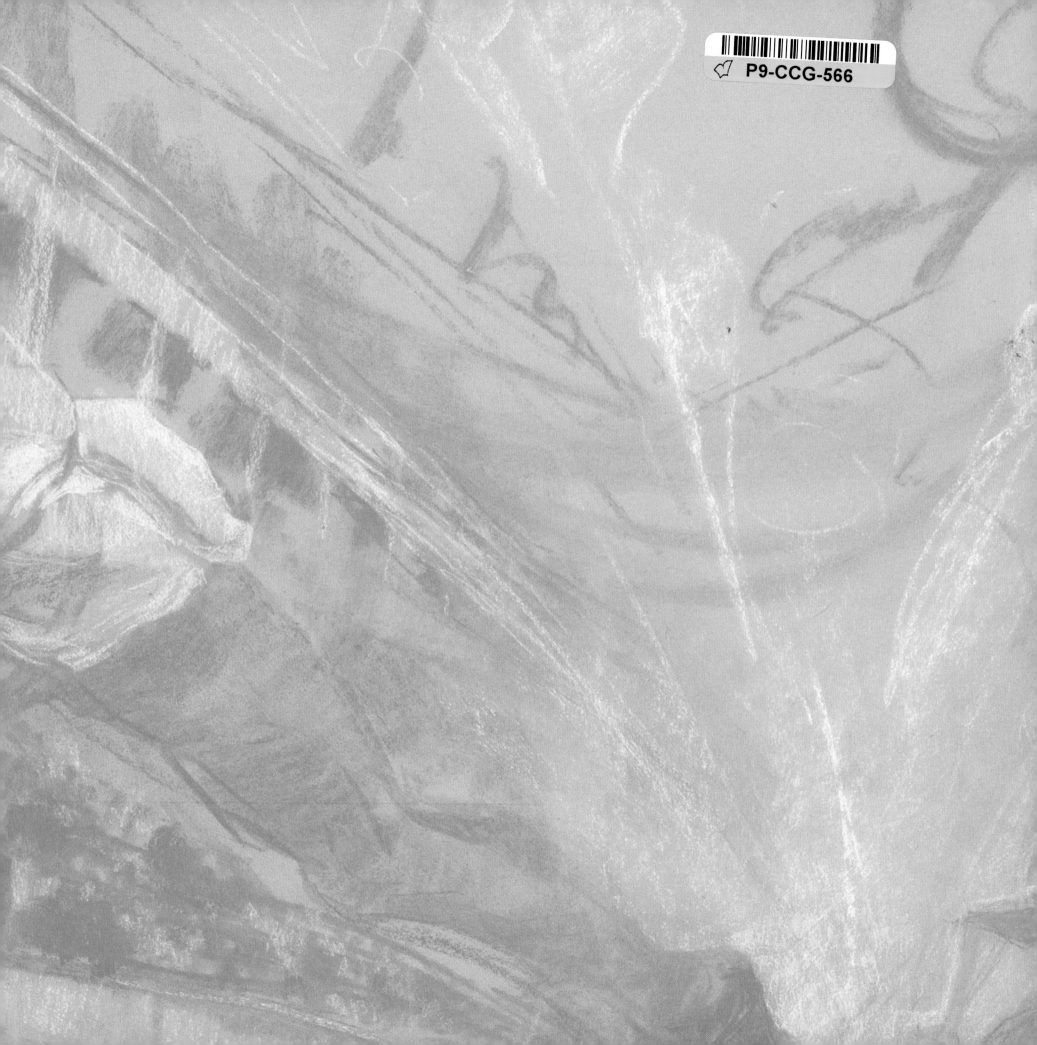

To four generations of great Black men who are storytellers and history makers:

Andrew Young, Sr. (Daddie Boo)

Andrew J. Young (Daddy)

Andrew Young III (Bo)

Andrew Jackson Young IV (Jack)

— P.Y.S.

To all the talented and hardworking generations of James and Cooper families who came before me.

— G.C.J.

Photos ©: 36 top and bottom: From the private collection of Andrew Young; 37: Associated Press/AP Images; background throughout: h.yegho/Shutterstock.
ISBN 978-0-545-55465-7 • 10 9 8 7 6 5 4 3 2 1   22 23 24 25 26
Printed in China   38 • First edition, August 2022
Book design by Doan Buu
The text type was set in Neutraface Text. The display type was set in Neutraface Text.
The illustrations were created using chalk pastels on Mi-Teintes pastel board with Adobe Photoshop used for finalization of the images.

JUST LIKE
JESSE OWENS

by Ambassador **Andrew Young**

as told to **Paula Young Shelton** • illustrated by **Gordon C. James**

Orchard Books
an Imprint of Scholastic Inc.
New York

I ran and ran. Head up, back straight, eyes focused, just like my daddy taught me. My feet pounded against the dirt. My heart pounded in my chest as I headed toward my target. I knew I could catch him. Jimmy Ray was bigger, but I was faster.

He tried to dodge me, but I was too quick.

"Tag! You're it!" I took off in the other direction. Jimmy Ray fell to the ground. He rolled over and jumped up, looking around for me. But I was gone, and there was no way he was gonna catch me.

Then J.D. started, "You'll never get me, yeah."

Jimmy Ray glanced his way. He knew J.D. was right. That country boy was used to running from alligators in the Louisiana swamps.

"Naa-naa-na-naa-naa," J.D. taunted.

That's when Jimmy Ray picked up a rock. "I bet I can knock your block off," he threatened.

We froze. I was pretty sure Jimmy Ray could do it. That boy had a good arm. He was always the first to get picked when we played baseball.

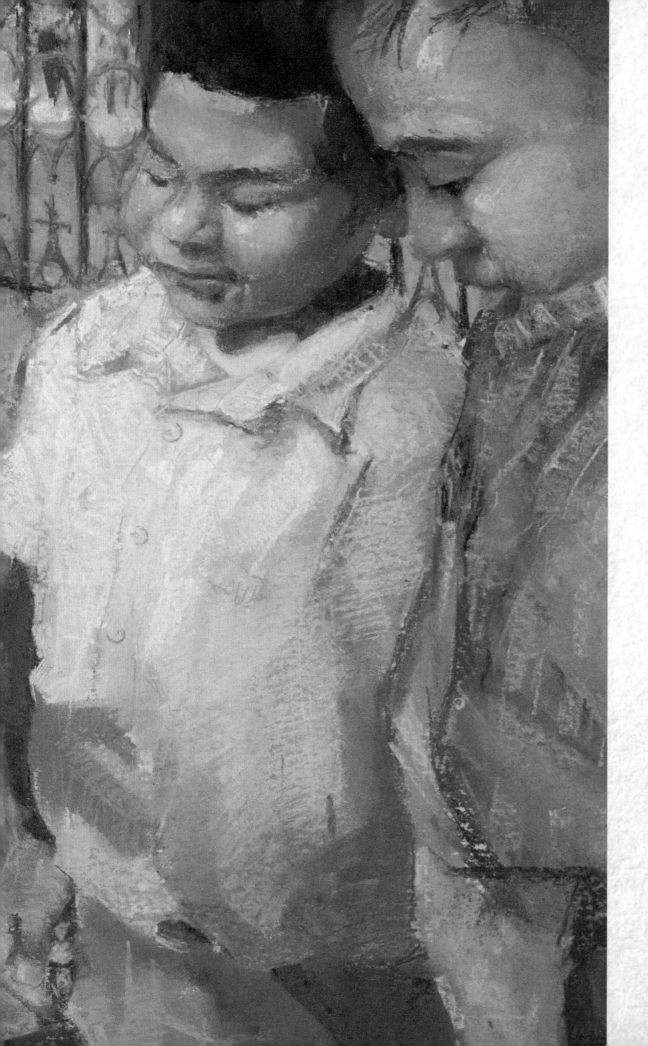

Luckily, just then our friend Norbie hopped over the old wooden fence. "Look what I've got here," he sang in his Irish accent.

There was a shiny new nickel in the palm of his hand. Everyone ran to see what he had, forgetting who was chasing who.

"Where'd you get that from?" I asked, as if I didn't know.

"My Aunt Ida paid me not to play with you, Andy." She was always telling him not to play with "those Colored boys," but Norbie didn't pay her no never mind.

See, there was segregation all over New Orleans — White folks on one side, Black folks on the other. But not on the playground, 'cause kids didn't care what color you were. What mattered most was how fast you could run and tag, how hard you could hit a baseball, or how far you could throw it.

So we kept on running, tagging, and throwing until suppertime.

"Andre-e-e-e-w-w!" I heard Mother call. I took off running right away. Mother did not like me to be late.

I hightailed it up the steps and walked inside. Where most people have a living room, we had a room filled with people waiting to get their teeth fixed. My daddy had a dental office that took up the front rooms of our house.

I went up to every last person in there, just like my daddy taught me, and with a firm handshake said, "Good afternoon." Daddy said it showed respect. Mother said it was just good home training.

"Go get Walter," Mother told me. "Your daddy and I have a meeting at the church tonight. Delia will take care of you."

I kissed Mother, grabbed my baby brother's hand, making sure to say "Good evening" to Daddy's last patients. Then Walter and I took off running to Aunt Delia's house a few doors down, head up, back straight, eyes focused. Aunt Delia was waiting for us at the door when we arrived.

We played cards while Aunt Delia cooked dinner. In the middle of our game, strange music started coming from the house behind us. I looked out the window and saw men standing at attention, each holding one arm stretched straight. They were singing in a language I didn't understand. It sounded like they were yelling, "Hi, Hitler!" It scared me so much, I nearly fell outta my seat.

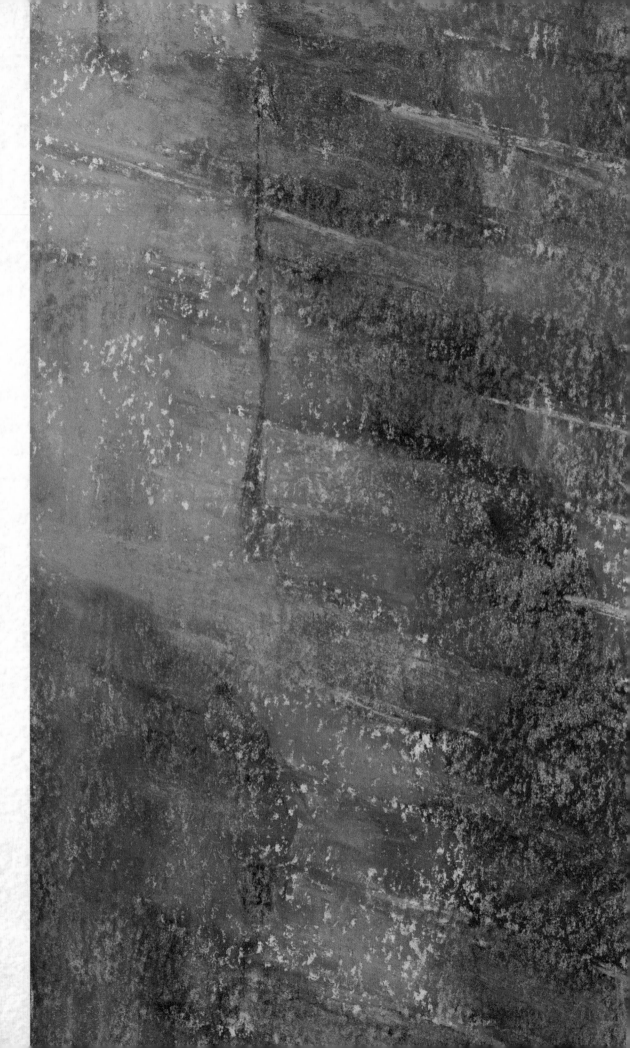

The next day, I told my friends all about what I'd seen. I even acted it out.

"That's nuts!" said Norbie, who copied my pose.

"Wonder if it's a new dance." J.D. tried to do a little jitterbug.

"Maybe they were playing flying aces," Jimmy Ray said. He put out both arms like an airplane and ran around in circles.

We all started running around pretending to be fighter jets until we heard our mothers calling us home for dinner.

When I got home, Daddy was walking two men to the door.

"Good evening, Mr. Berman, Mr. Stern."

They were salesmen who sold Daddy his dental supplies. They were the only White people who'd show their faces here in broad daylight (though sometimes White customers would sneak in at night). They were talking kind of loud as they walked down the steps.

"Dr. Young, how can you live with those savages down the street? They think they're better than you and me. That Hitler is doing terrible things to my people in Germany, and they think he should run the world! If you weren't such a good customer, I wouldn't step foot in this neighborhood!"

That evening, after the last patient left, Daddy and I went out to the sidewalk to play catch. I tossed the ball and asked, "Daddy, what's Hitler?"

Daddy paused, then tossed the ball back with his own question, "Why do you ask, Andrew?"

"Well, I saw soldiers saying 'hi' to Hitler behind Aunt Delia's house, and then Mr. Berman and Mr. Stern were talking about him too."

I caught the ball as Daddy answered, "Hitler is the chancellor of Germany. He's like the president. And they weren't saying 'hi,' they were saying 'heil' — a German word that means hail — to salute and honor Hitler."

"Why would they salute the almost-president of Germany when he wasn't even there?" I tossed the ball back.

Daddy didn't answer me at first. Finally, he threw me a grounder and said, "Hitler believes White Christians are better than everyone else. So he doesn't care much for Colored folks like us, or Jewish people like Mr. Berman and Mr. Stern. Hitler's followers are showing they agree with him by saluting."

I threw the ball straight into Daddy's glove and asked, "Why do they think they're better than us?"

Daddy immediately popped a fly ball back. "Because they're sick. Racism is a sickness. We've got to help folks like that."

I caught the pop fly and stared back at my daddy. "How do we do that?"

"Well, you can start by just being the best person you can be. That's why we practice baseball, and why Mother makes you do your homework, and why we tell you to be polite and greet everyone. This will show others that it doesn't matter what color your skin is. It's what you do that counts."

The next Saturday, Daddy and I got all dressed up in our Sunday best, and we took the streetcar downtown to the Orpheum Theater for a special treat.

We walked around the side of the theater and down an alley to the window marked "Colored." We bought two tickets.

Then Daddy took my hand as we went in the back door and climbed the steps to the balcony to sit in the "Colored Only" section. I didn't like that we had to go in through the back and sit in the balcony, when we paid the same amount as White folks who went in the front door and sat where they wanted to.

Once we were inside the theater, I didn't care where we sat. It was beautiful. I looked up and the ceiling was covered with gold, red, and blue shapes. Suddenly, the lights went out, the projector flashed on, and a loud voice boomed out through the speakers.

A Movietone newsreel flickered on the screen. It was highlights from the 1936 Olympics in Germany. There was that man called Hitler with his funny little mustache and a stadium full of people who stood up to salute him. They looked just like those men outside Aunt Delia's window. The athletes in the film ran, jumped, and threw as the crowds applauded. The best part of the whole film was Jesse Owens, a runner who looked like me, winning over and over and over again.

I cheered as Jesse pulled way ahead of the pack in the 100-meter dash and won a gold medal.

I shouted as Jesse flew through the air and leaped over the sand to nab a gold medal in the long jump.

I screamed as Jesse raced past the others in the 200 meters for yet another gold.

I roared as Jesse took the lead and passed the baton to help bring the Americans victory and win gold again in the 4x100-meter relay.

I saw Jesse Owens run — head up, back straight, eyes focused — on to victory, to win four gold medals in front of a man who thought people like me were not as good as White people.

The next day I couldn't wait to get back to the playground. I ran like Jesse Owens to see my friends. I told them all about the movie theater, and how Hitler thought White people were the best, and how Jesse Owens proved him wrong by running faster and jumping farther than everybody else.

Jimmy Ray, Norbie, J.D., and I ran and ran and ran that day like we were in the Olympics and nobody cared what color we were. After seeing Jesse win, I decided I would play harder, work harder, and try harder than ever to be the best I could be. And I would show the world that it doesn't matter what color you are. What matters is what you do. All people deserve a chance to go for the gold, just like Jesse.

Author's Note

My father, Andrew Young, is a storyteller who uses stories to teach valuable lessons. He and I wanted to share this story about his experience with Jesse Owens, and agreed that the best way to do so was for me to write it as Daddy told it to me, taking some artistic license with the dialogue. I've heard this story throughout my life, along with my siblings, Andrea, Lisa, and Bo. I have recounted it based on conversations with Daddy, as well as research.

My father grew up in a diverse neighborhood in New Orleans when there was legal segregation throughout the South and racial inequity across America. In this story, I use the term "Colored" to describe people of African descent. This term reflects the speech of the 1930s. My grandfather, who we called Daddie Boo, often told my father and his brother, Walter, that when dealing with the sickness of racism, "Don't get mad, get smart."

Daisy, Andrew Sr., Andrew, Walter
circa 1944

My sister, Lisa (left), our father, Andrew Young, and me at the Poor People's Campaign, 1968.

Daddie Boo took my father to the local movie theater to see newsreels of Jesse Owens running in the 1936 Olympics to show how important it is to lead by example. Adolf Hitler was eager to host the Olympics in Germany to show the world that blond, blue-eyed Aryans were the superior race. When Jesse Owens won four gold medals, he proved Hitler wrong. At the same time, Jesse showed that working harder and smarter was better than fighting.

My father used Daddie Boo's lessons to guide his life. Even as he marched alongside Martin Luther King, Jr., to gain equal rights for Blacks and was beaten unconscious, he didn't get angry; instead, he continued to stand up for what was right. Sixty years after he saw Jesse Owens run, Daddy worked with the leadership of the city to bring the 1996 Centennial Olympic Games to Atlanta.

— *Paula Young Shelton*

Illustrator's Note

I see myself in Andrew Young's story. Growing up in Fort Washington, Maryland, I had friends of many different ethnicities. It was a great place to spend my childhood, but as a kid, I knew that some of my friends' parents thought less of me because of my blackness. To combat this and prepare us for the world outside our loving home, my parents, Thomas and Beatrice James, poured all they had worked for into my sister and me. To enlarge our creative lives, Mom and Dad took us to the Smithsonian Institution and the Kennedy Center for the Performing Arts to see paintings, theater, and concerts. Like Andrew Young and countless African American children, I was told I'd have to be better than the best to prove myself in the world. To this end, my parents supported my journey as an artist. As a college graduation gift, Mom and Dad made a meaningful investment in my future by purchasing an expensive 250-piece set of Sennelier soft pastels. The pastels are creamy and vibrant — like butter on paper when I draw.

For twenty years, I kept those precious pastels in their box, waiting for the perfect project and reason to crack open the gift my parents had provided. Two decades later, when I read Paula Young Shelton's powerful retelling of her father's childhood story, I knew this could serve as a meaningful tribute to my parents and all they have done for me as a Black artist. Using the pastels for the first time is my way of continuing the legacy of excellence my parents instilled in me, that Andrew Young fostered in children of all races, and that inspired Jesse Owens to prove, by example, that the best way to make a difference is to win.

— *Gordon C. James*

Jesse Owens
Berlin Olympics 1936

Jesse Owens

James Cleveland "Jesse" Owens specialized in sprints and the long jump. He set three world records and tied another, all in less than an hour, at the 1935 Big Ten track meet in Ann Arbor, Michigan — a feat that has never been equaled and has been referred to as the greatest 45 minutes ever in sports. His achievement at the 1936 Summer Olympics skyrocketed him to international fame, but Jesse will always be a one-of-a-kind athlete.